We Work at the

Hospital

Angela Aylmore

Heinemann Library
Chicago, Illinois

© 2006 Heinemann Library
a division of Reed Elsevier Inc.
Chicago, Illinois

Customer Service   888-454-2279
Visit our website at www.heinemannlibrary.com

Photo research by Erica Newbery
Designed by Jo Hinton-Malivoire and bigtop
Printed in China by South China Printing Company

10 09 08 07 06
10 9 8 7 6 5 4 3 2 1

Library of Congress Cataloging-in-Publication Data
Aylmore, Angela.
  We work in a hospital / Angela Aylmore.
      p. cm. -- (Where we work)
  Includes bibliographical references and index.
  ISBN 1-4109-2246-4 (library binding - hardcover) -- ISBN 1-4109-2251-0 (pbk.)
  1. Hospitals--Medical staff--Juvenile literature. 2. Hospitals--Staff--Juvenile literature. 3. Hospitals--Juvenile literature. I. Title. II. Series.
RA972.A95 2006
362.11068'3--dc22
                                        2005033529

Acknowledgments
The publishers would like to thank the following for permission to reproduce photographs:
Alamy pp. **18** (Janine Wiedel Photolibrary), **20** (Medical-on-Line); Corbis p. **21** (Jim Craigmyle); Getty Images pp. **4–5** (Photodisc), **6–7** (Taxi), **8**, **10–11** (Taxi/Gary Buss), **11** bottom (Photodisc), **12** (Photodisc/Keith Brofsky), **13** (Photodisc), **15** (Stone/Charles Thatcher); Photos.com pp. **16**, **17**, **19**; Stockbyte Royalty Free Photos pp. **8–9**. Quiz pp. **22–23**: **astronaut** (Getty/Photodisc), **brush and comb** (Corbis/DK Limited), **doctor** (Getty Images/Photodisc), **firefighter helmet** (Corbis), **ladder** (Corbis/Royalty Free), **scrubs** (Corbis), **space food** (Alamy/Hugh Threlfall), **stethoscope** (Getty Images/Photodisc), **thermometer** (Getty Images/Photodisc).

Cover photograph of a doctor reproduced with permission of Stockbyte Royalty Free Photos.

Every effort has been made to contact copyright holders of any material reproduced in this book. Any omissions will be rectified in subsequent printings if notice is given to the publisher. The paper used to print this book comes from sustainable resources.

Some words are shown in bold, **like this**. They are explained in the glossary on page 24.

Contents

Welcome to the Hospital!

This is a hospital.

People come here
when they are sick
or injured.

Working in a Hospital

Lots of people work in a hospital.

It is a very
busy place.

7

8

We drive people to the hospital in an **ambulance**.

9

The Doctor

I am a doctor. I find out why you are sick.

This **stethoscope** helps me listen to your heart.

The Nurse

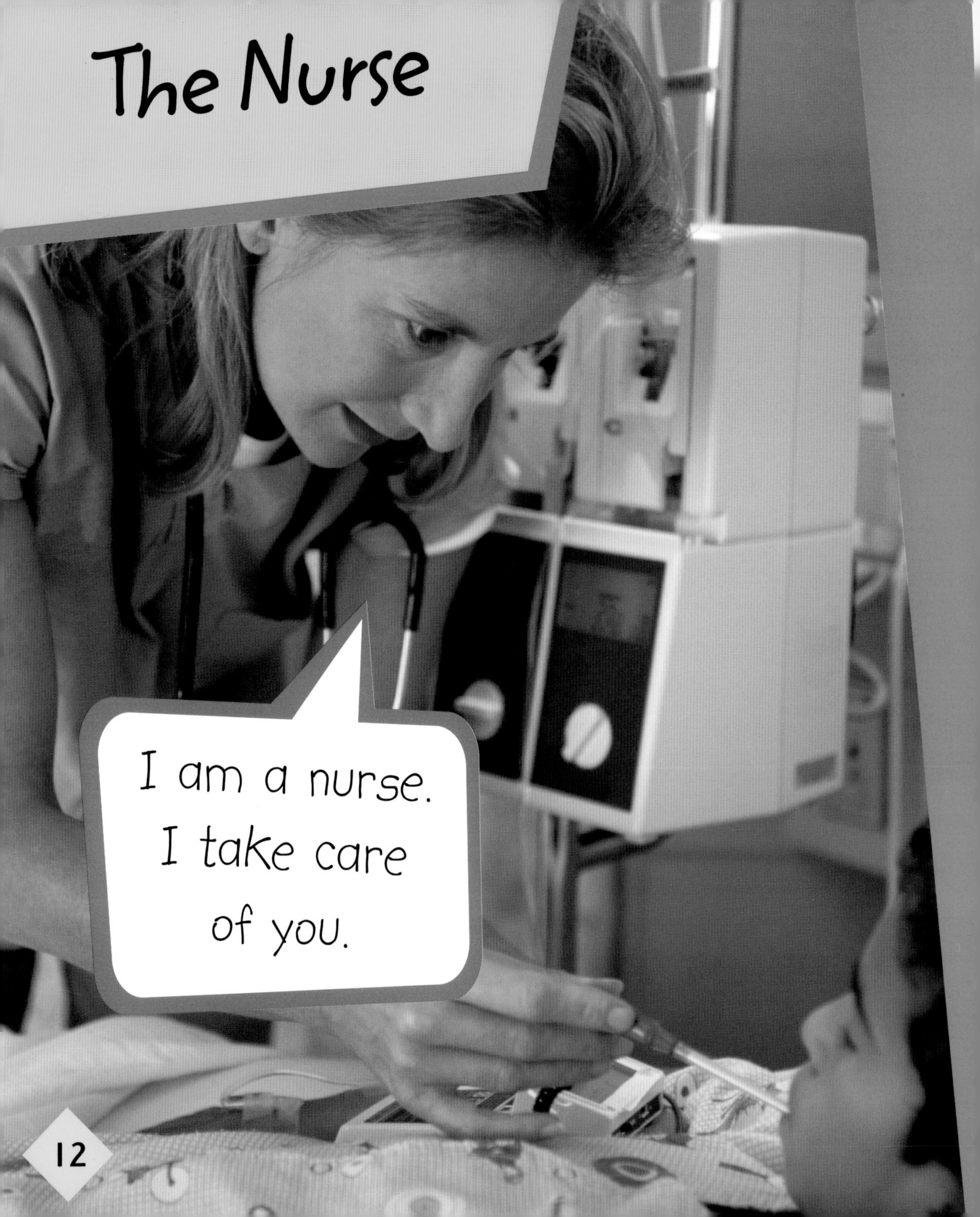

This **thermometer** helps me take your **temperature**.

The Surgeon

In an **operation** I wear gloves and a mask.

They stop me from giving you **germs**.

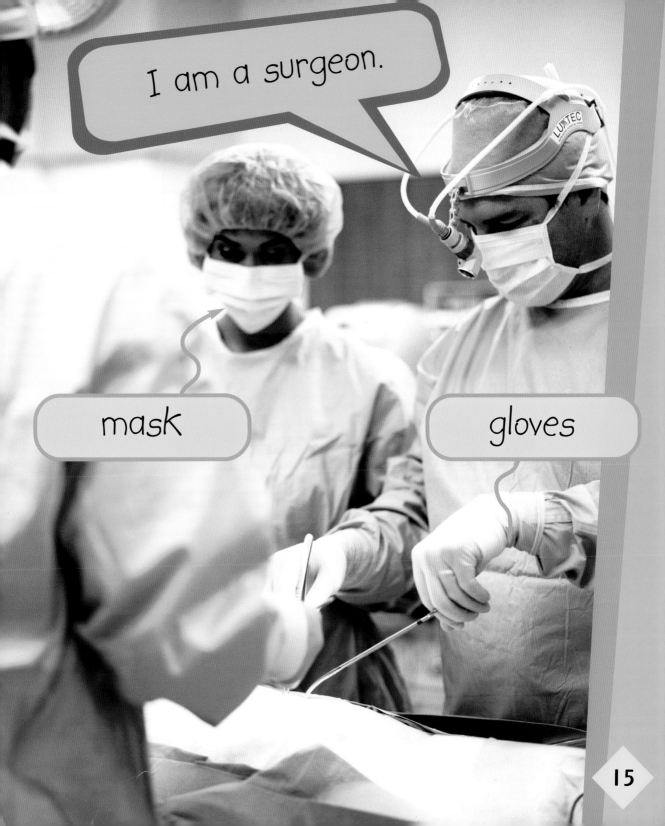

Hospital Uniforms

doctor

We wear **uniforms** in the hospital.

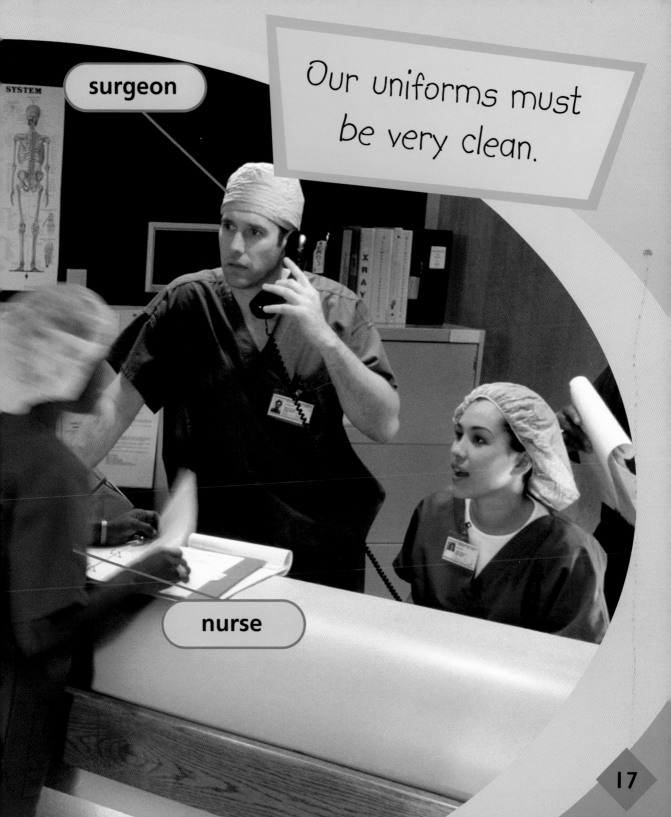

Special Tools

This is an
X-ray machine.

It takes pictures of your bones.

Getting better

We mend broken bones by putting them in a cast.

We are always happy
when we can make
someone better!

Quiz

space food

Do you want to be a nurse or doctor? Which of these things would you need?

stethoscope

spacesuit

helmet

ladder

combs and
brushes

nurse's uniform

white coat

thermometer

23

Glossary

ambulance special truck that takes people to hospital

germs things in the air that can make you ill

operation a way of making a person better

stethoscope what a doctor uses to listen to your heart beat

temperature how hot you are.

thermometer what a nurse uses to take your temperature

uniform special clothes the doctors and nurses wear at work

Index

Notes for Adults

This series supports the young child's exploration of their learning environment and their knowledge and understanding of their world.

The series shows the different jobs that professionals do in four different environments. There are opportunities to compare and contrast the jobs and provide an understanding of what each entails.

The books will help the child to extend their vocabulary, as they will hear new words. Some of the words that may be new to them in **We Work at the Hospital** are *operation, germs, thermometer, temperature,* and *stethoscope*. Since the words are used in context in the book, this should enable the young child to gradually incorporate them into their own vocabulary.

Follow-up Activities
The child could role play situations in a hospital. Areas could be set up to create a waiting room, operating room, or ambulance. The child could also record what they have found out by drawing, painting, or tape recording their experiences.